THE
MAGNIFICENT
BOOK
OF
CATS

THE
MAGNIFICENT
BOOK
OF
CATS

ILLUSTRATED BY
Andrew Beckett &
Simon Treadwell

WRITTEN BY
Barbara Taylor

weldonowen

Written by Barbara Taylor
Illustrated by Andrew Beckett and Simon Treadwell

weldon**owen**

Copyright © Weldon Owen Children's Books, 2023

Published by Weldon Owen Children's Books
An imprint of Weldon Owen International, L.P.
A subsidiary of Insight International, L.P.
PO Box 3088
San Rafael, CA 94912
www.insighteditions.com

Weldon Owen Children's Books:
Designed by Bryn Walls
Edited by Diana Craig
Senior Production Manager: Greg Steffen
Art Director: Stuart Smith
Publisher: Sue Grabham

Insight Editions:
Publisher: Raoul Goff

ISBN: 978-1-68188-886-6
Manufactured, printed and assembled in China
First printing, October 2022. TOP1022
26 25 24 23 22 1 2 3 4 5

MIX
Paper from
responsible sources
FSC® C104723

Introduction

There are more than 500 million domestic (pet or working) cats living all over the world. Cats began to live with people around 10,000 years ago, when we started to farm the land. Wildcats were welcome because they hunted the rats and mice feeding on people's grain stores. Tamed cats were taken aboard sailing ships as rat catchers, and they spread widely across the globe. People crossbred them to create pedigree breeds with different coats, characteristics, and personalities.

The Magnificent Book of Cats introduces us to some of the world's most wonderful and incredible cat breeds. Meet the Turkish Angora, who can open doors and turn on taps, and the Abyssinian that can run faster than an Olympic human sprinter. Spot the curly-haired Devon Rex and the Bengal that looks like a miniature leopard. Learn about the floppy Ragdoll, the hairless Peterbald, and the short-legged Munchkin, named after the characters in the story *The Wizard of Oz*.

Meet some other amazing breeds too, such as the Savannah that can leap over fences nearly six times its own height. Discover the Siberian, with its waterproof coat, and the Norwegian Forest Cat, whose furry paws work like snowshoes.

Get ready to enter the magnificent realm of cats as you explore some of the most fascinating breeds from around the world.

Fact file

Originates: France

Group: Shorthair

Height: 8–11 in./20–28 cm

Weight: 6–9 lb./2.7–4 kg (female); 10–14 lb./4.5–6.8 kg (male)

Color: Gray-blue

Contents

Bengal

 The Bengal cat looks like a mini-leopard. It was specially bred to look this way by crossing domestic house cats with wild leopard cats from Asia.

 Bengals are more like dogs than most other domestic cats. They like to play games of fetch or chase. They will even go for walks on the end of a leash.

 Many pet cats hate water, but Bengals love it. They like to play in water, and some even like to swim.

 These strong, energetic, and athletic animals are larger than the typical pet cat. Bengals are good at jumping and climbing, like their leopard cat ancestors.

Fact file

Originates: Asia, USA

Group: Shorthair

Height: 13–16 in./33–40.6 cm

Weight: 8–12 lb./3.6–5.4 kg (female); 10–15 lb./4.5–6.8 kg (male)

Color: Various with spots or marbling, or all-black

Bengal cats make all sorts of sounds, from growling and howling to meowing and purring. Sometimes they purr so loudly, they can be heard from another room.

The Bengal's luxurious fur may be spotted or marbled with swirly stripes. It may also have a rosette pattern, like the rings on a leopard's coat. Bengals are the only domestic cats with these rosettes.

Just like wild leopards, some Bengal cats have an all-black coat. They still have spots or marbling, but these patterns only show up when the light strikes their fur in a certain way.

Russian Blue

 Russian Blue kittens are born with yellow eyes. As they grow, their eyes change to a striking emerald-green color. Most kittens start with blue eyes, which later become brown or yellow.

 This breed developed its thick, velvety fur to help keep it warm in the freezing Russian winter. Its coat has two layers—a soft, feathery undercoat and a silky top coat, which shimmers in the light.

 In the 1800s, sailors from the port of Arkhangelsk (Archangel) in Russia may have taken Russian Blues on board ship with them. This is why these cats are sometimes called Archangel Blues.

 Most domestic cats have gray paw pads, but the pads of a Russian Blue are mauve or lavender in color.

 In old legends, Russian Blues were said to be lucky cats with magical healing powers. People once kept them near their newborn babies to protect the infants from evil spirits and bad luck.

Russian Blues are very muscular, athletic cats that like to jump and climb. Their long legs allow them to run at high speed.

 The slightly upturned mouth of a Russian Blue makes the cat look as if it is gently smiling.

Fact file

Originates: Russia

Group: Shorthair

Height: 9–11 in./23–28 cm

Weight: 7–10 lb./3–4.5 kg (female); 10–12 lb./4.5–5.4 kg (male)

Color: Blue-gray

Somali

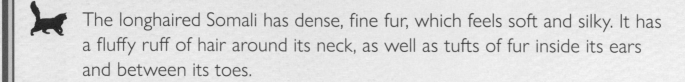

The longhaired Somali has dense, fine fur, which feels soft and silky. It has a fluffy ruff of hair around its neck, as well as tufts of fur inside its ears and between its toes.

The Somali has been nicknamed "the fox cat" because of its bushy tail.

Somalis have a finely speckled or "ticked" coat. This is because each hair is striped in bands of different colors, with black at the tip. There can be between six and twenty-four bands on each hair.

A Somali's ears are large and pointed. Its big, almond-shaped eyes can be green, amber, or copper in color. A dark ring surrounds each eye, as if it has been outlined with black eyeliner.

These athletic and energetic cats are always on the move and love to explore. They may try to open cupboards, swipe things out of drawers, and turn on taps.

Somalis can learn to hold objects and food in their paws, rather like a monkey.

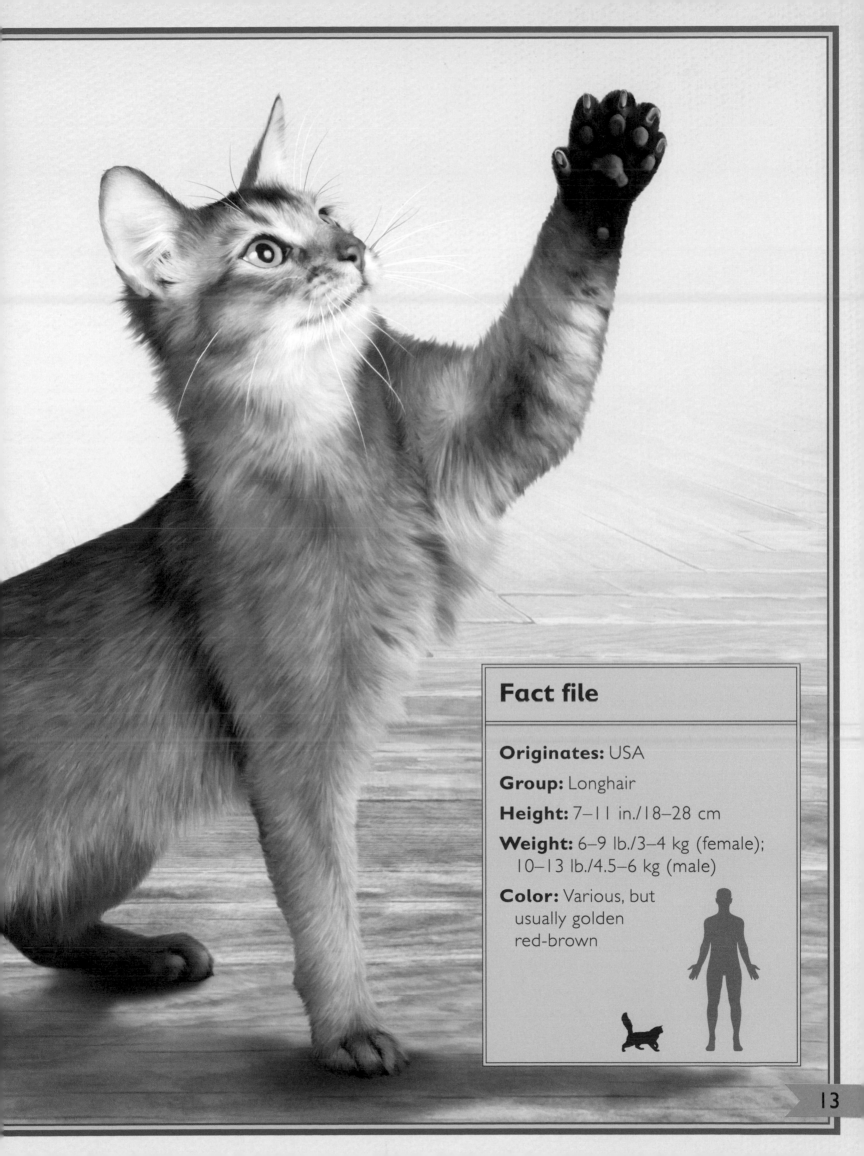

Fact file

Originates: USA

Group: Longhair

Height: 7–11 in./18–28 cm

Weight: 6–9 lb./3–4 kg (female); 10–13 lb./4.5–6 kg (male)

Color: Various, but usually golden red-brown

American Shorthair

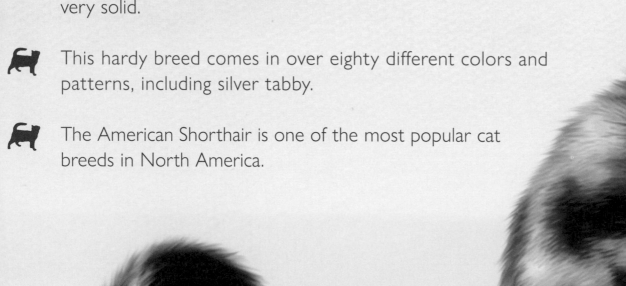

American Shorthairs are descended from cats that arrived in North America more than 400 years ago. These cats came on sailing ships. Their job was to kill the rats and mice on board.

The American Shorthair has a thick, dense coat that keeps it extra warm.

The sturdy American Shorthair has a broad chest, thick neck, powerful legs, wide muzzle, and strong jaws. Heavy muscles and bones make this cat feel very solid.

This hardy breed comes in over eighty different colors and patterns, including silver tabby.

The American Shorthair is one of the most popular cat breeds in North America.

These large, athletic, muscular cats are known for their strength, endurance, and balance. They are also excellent hunters.

 This Shorthair is a quiet cat that does not meow a lot, unlike some other breeds.

Fact file

Originates: USA

Group: Shorthair

Height: 8–10 in./20–25 cm

Weight: 8–13 lb./3.6–6 kg (female); 11–15 lb./5–7 kg (male)

Color: Various

Sphynx

🐁 A Sphynx cat has no whiskers or eyelashes and may look as if it is completely bald. In fact, its body does have a thin coat of fine, soft, fuzzy hair.

🐁 This cat has very sensitive skin, which gets sunburned easily. The markings on its body are caused by pigments, or colorings, in its skin.

🐁 The Sphynx got its name because it looks like the Great Sphinx in Egypt. This statue has the body of a lion and a human head, and guards the Egyptian pyramids.

🐁 This breed has no thick fur to keep it warm, but its high body temperature protects it from the cold. The body of a Sphynx is several degrees warmer than that of other cats.

🐁 Sphynx cats need a lot of food to give them fuel and to help generate body heat.

🐁 The Sphynx has saggy, wrinkled skin on its head, body, and legs. This makes it hard for the cat to groom itself thoroughly. Its skin also produces a lot of greasy oil. A Sphynx's owners usually need to bathe it to keep it smelling fresh and clean.

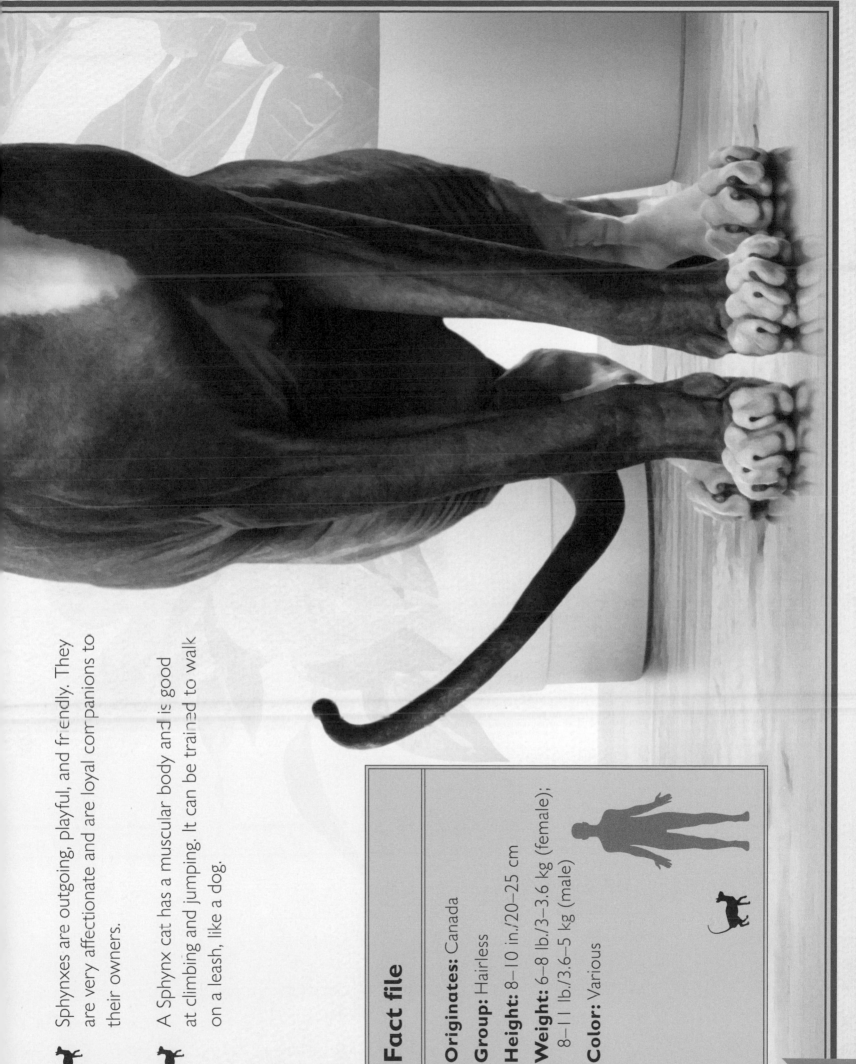

- Sphynxes are outgoing, playful, and friendly. They are very affectionate and are loyal companions to their owners.

- A Sphynx cat has a muscular body and is good at climbing and jumping. It can be trained to walk on a leash, like a dog.

Fact file

Originates: Canada

Group: Hairless

Height: 8–10 in./20–25 cm

Weight: 6–8 lb./3–3.6 kg (female); 8–11 lb./3.6–5 kg (male)

Color: Various

Turkish Angora

The highly intelligent Turkish Angora is easy to train and is clever enough to solve problems. It can even learn how to open doors and turn on taps with its small, furry paws.

As well as a beautiful snowy white, Angoras come in a variety of colors and patterns, including tortoiseshell and tabby stripes. Its fur doesn't reach its full length until the cat is about two years old.

Angoras often have eyes of different colors, such as one blue eye and one gold eye. Their eyes are shaped like almonds.

The Turkish Angora was named after the Turkish city of Angora. Today, this city is called Ankara.

Turkish Angoras like water, which is unusual for a cat. They are usually excellent swimmers..

Fact file

Originates: Turkey

Group: Longhair

Height: 9–14 in./23–35.5 cm

Weight: 5–8 lb./2.5–4 kg (female); 7–10 lb./3.5–5 kg (male)

Color: Various

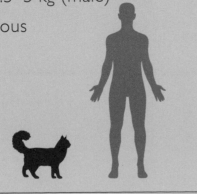

This strong, muscular, agile cat moves like a graceful ballerina. It is good at climbing and loves to run around and play, even when it an adult.

 Angoras are friendly, determined, and outgoing cats. They like to "talk" to their owners.

 The beautiful Angora was the favorite cat of the famous French queen Marie Antoinette, who lived around 250 years ago. She had six pet Angora cats.

Burmese

The friendly and energetic Burmese has a mischievous personality. It is sometimes called "the dog cat" because it loves to play games of fetch, tag, and hide-and-seek. It can also obey commands such as "Sit" and "Roll over."

A female cat called Wong Mau was an ancestor of this breed. She lived in Burma but was taken to America, where she was mated with a Siamese cat. Their offspring were the first "Burmese" cats.

In Burma, the ancestors of this breed were kept as sacred animals in temples and monasteries. They were known as "copper cats" because of the rich red-brown color of their coat.

Burmese cats have coats that are as smooth and glossy as silk.

Like their Siamese cousins, Burmese cats are very curious, and demand a lot of attention. The sound they make is a like a soft, raspy rumble.

 Burmese cats are excellent climbers and jumpers. They often leap up onto a high shelf or windowsill, where they can perch to watch the world go by.

 Male and female Burmese often have different personalities. Males tend to be quieter and less active. Females can be more curious and want to be involved with everything their owners are doing.

Fact file

Originates: Burma (present-day Myanmar), USA

Group: Shorthair

Height: 10–12 in./25–30 cm

Weight: 8–10 lb./3.5–4.5 kg (female); 9–12 lb./4–5.5 kg (male)

Color: Various

Ragdoll

- The friendly Ragdoll is an easygoing, relaxed cat. When picked up, it goes all floppy like an old-fashioned ragdoll toy with its loose, floppy arms and legs.

- Ragdolls are supersized. The male is one of the largest of all domestic cats, with big bones. It can weigh almost as much as a medium-sized dog.

- Most Ragdolls have two sparkling blue eyes. But some have one eye in another color, such as green. The ear on the same side as their blue eye may be deaf.

- These cats like lots of cuddles and attention, and often follow their owners about, or greet them at the front door. They are like puppies and love playing with toys.

- A Ragdoll's fur is long and silky, and comes in many colors. A typical Ragdoll has a white or cream body with a darker color, such as brown, on its face, tail, ears, and legs.

- Most Ragdoll kittens are white when they are born. Their other colors start to appear during the first few weeks of life.

The Ragdoll doesn't reach its adult size and gain its full coloring until it is three or four years old.

This cat's long fur does not get knotted easily because it does not have much of an undercoat. It also doesn't shed its fur as much as other cats.

Fact file

Originates: USA

Group: Semi-longhair to longhair

Height: 9–11 in./23–28 cm

Weight: 10–15 lb./4.5–6.8 kg (female); 15–20 lb./6.8–9 kg (male)

Color: Various and tortoiseshell or tabby coat patterns

Maine Coon

 This friendly, gentle giant is the biggest domestic cat. The longest Maine Coon measured 4 feet (1.2 m) from its nose to the tip of its tail. That's the height of an average seven-year-old child.

 The Maine Coon comes from the state of Maine. It was called "coon" because people wrongly believed it was related to raccoons, which have shaggy fur and big, bushy, striped tails.

 This cat's long, thick, waterproof fur helps to keep it warm and dry in cold winters. Shaggy fur on its belly and back legs protects it when it walks over snow or ice, and its furry paws act like snowshoes.

 The Maine Coon's fluffy tail is at least as long as its back. The cat curls the tail around its face and shoulders like a big, snuggly scarf for extra warmth and protection against the cold.

Fact file

Originates: USA

Group: Longhair

Height: 8–16 in./20–41 cm

Weight: 8–15 lb./3.6–6.8 kg (female); 13–25 lb./6–11.3 kg (male)

Color: Various solid colors, tabby and tortoiseshell patterns

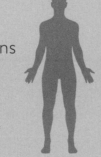

This active, muscular breed has lots of energy and is very playful. It likes to chase and fetch toys and play with water..

Maine Coons love being with people and often follow them around.

Munchkin

 The Munchkin cat has extremely short, stubby legs. They are about half as long as the legs of other domestic cats.

 This breed was named after the people called Munchkins in the classic novel and film, *The Wizard of Oz*.

 A Munchkin called Lilieput is the world's shortest cat. She is only 5.25 inches (13.34 cm) tall from the ground to the top of her shoulders. This is only slightly taller than a can of soup.

 Munchkins like to hide their favorite toys and other objects to play with later. They are especially fond of shiny objects.

Fact file

Originates: USA

Group: Shorthair or longhair

Height: 5–9 in./13–23 cm

Weight: 4–8 lb./2–3.6 kg (female); 6–9 lb./3–4 kg (male)

Color: Various

The Munchkin sometimes raises itself up on its back legs to get a better view, like a rabbit or a meerkat.

Despite its short legs, the Munchkin runs quickly. It can zoom around corners easily, like a racing car, because its body is close to the ground.

Siberian

The Siberian cat has a superthick coat with three layers of glossy fur. It also has a thick, furry neck ruff, extra-furry ears, and large, furry paws.

Some cat experts think that the Siberian cat may be the ancestor of all today's longhaired cat breeds, including the Angora, the Norwegian Forest Cat, and the Persian cat.

Unlike most other cats, Siberians like playing with water. Their top coat is waterproof.

The easygoing, gentle Siberian is a very loyal pet and tends to follow its owners around. It loves human company and sometimes greets visitors at the door.

Siberians "talk" to their owners with a variety of trills, chirps, growls, meows, and purrs.

These cats are expert hunters. Russian farmers used them to keep rats and mice away from their stores of grain and other foodstuffs.

The Siberian has been a domestic cat in Russia for hundreds of years. It even features in Russian fairy tales. The Siberian is the national cat of Russia.

Fact file

Originates: Russia

Group: Semi-longhair

Height: 9–11 in./23–28 cm

Weight: 13–17 lb/5.9–7.7 kg (female); 17–26 lb./7.7–11.8 kg (male)

Color: Various

Savannah

 The leggy Savannah looks like a wildcat but is friendly and tame. The breed was created by crossing a wild African serval cat with a domestic Siamese cat.

 Savannahs are the world's tallest domestic cat. They can be as big as a medium-sized dog.

 The adventurous Savannah can leap an amazing 8 feet (2.5 m) or more straight up from the ground—that's higher than an average door.

Fact file

Originates: Africa, USA

Group: Shorthair

Height: 14–17 in./35.5–43 cm

Weight: 8–12 lb./3.6–5.4 kg (female); 23–30 lb./10.4–13.6 kg (male)

Color: Brown or gray with black spots, black

The Savannah may wag its tail like a dog when greeting people.

 Savannahs are highly intelligent. They get bored easily and then become restless. These clever cats need plenty of toys and activities to challenge their big brains.

Korat

 The Korat is one of the oldest cat breeds in the world.

 This cat's big, round eyes are one of its most striking features. These are blue at birth but gradually change to amber, fringed with green. By two to four years, a Korat's eyes are completely green.

 The Korat's fine, glossy coat has silver-tipped hairs, making its fur shimmer in the light. This is one of the few cat breeds that come in only one color—a silvery blue-gray.

 The Korat's Thai nickname is *si-sawat*, which means "color of the sawat seed." This seed is a grayish-blue color, just like the cat's fur.

 In Thai tradition, the Korat is a lucky cat. An ancient Thai manuscript called *The Book of Cat Poems* lists the Korat as one of several breeds that will bring good fortune.

 A pair of Korat cats is a traditional gift to a bride at a Thai wedding.

Fact file

Originates: Thailand

Group: Shorthair

Length: 10–12 in./25–30 cm

Weight: 5–9 lb./2.2–4 kg (female); 9–11 lb./4–5 kg (male)

Color: Blue-gray

Oriental Shorthair

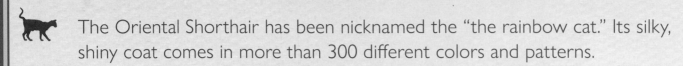

The Oriental Shorthair has been nicknamed the "the rainbow cat." Its silky, shiny coat comes in more than 300 different colors and patterns.

This friendly cat loves human company. It doesn't like being left on its own for long periods.

The almond-shaped eyes of the Oriental Shorthair may be green or blue. Some Oriental Shorthairs have odd-colored eyes, with one green and one blue eye.

The Oriental Shorthair is an elegant cat with long, slender legs, dainty oval paws, and a long, whiplike tail that tapers to a point.

The loyal Oriental Shorthair is very fond of its human owners and tends to follow them around. It "talks" to them a lot, meowing in a loud, raspy voice.

This highly intelligent cat enjoys being the center of attention at all times. It needs games, puzzles, and toys to play with, and easily learns new tricks, such as jumping through hoops.

A graceful and agile cat, the Oriental Shorthair is a champion climber and jumper. Its muscular body and long back legs give it athletic power.

Fact file

Originates: Thailand, USA, UK

Group: Shorthair

Height: 9–11 in./23–28 cm

Weight: 5–8 lb./2.2–3.6 kg (female);
8–12 lb./3.6–5.4 kg (male)

Color: Various

Persian

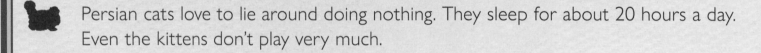

Persian cats love to lie around doing nothing. They sleep for about 20 hours a day. Even the kittens don't play very much.

The hairs in a Persian's flowing coat are 4–6 inches (10–15 cm) long. Even its ears and paws have tufts of long hair. A Persian's coat needs daily brushing to stop the fur becoming tangled and matted.

Persians have flat, slightly scrunched-up faces with large, expressive eyes, tiny button noses, and small, triangular mouths.

The gentle, friendly Persian enjoys being stroked and fussed over. It also "talks" to its owner a lot using a singsong meow.

Persian cats have been around for thousands of years. A cat that looks like a Persian appeared in ancient Eqyptian hieroglyphics over 3,000 years ago.

The James Bond villain Ernst Blofield had a white Persian cat that he stroked while it sat on his lap.

Fact file

Originates: Persia (modern-day Iran)

Group: Longhair

Height: 10–15 in./25–38 cm

Weight: 7–10 lb./3–4.5 kg (female); 9–13 lb./4–6 kg (male)

Color: Various

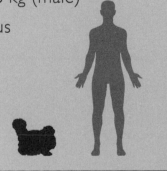

Manx

 Manx cats don't have long tails like other cats. In fact, they may not have a tail at all. Manxes without tails are called "rumpies." "Stumpies" have stumpy tails. "Longies" have longer tails, but these are still really short.

 The Manx takes its name from the Isle of Man, off the coast of Britain. The breed may have originated there. Or it may be descended from ships' cats with no tails that sailors accidentally brought to the island.

 Unlike most other cats, the Manx cannot use its tail for balance. Instead, it relies on its powerful round rump, or rear part of its body, to help it balance when it jumps.

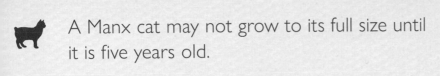 A Manx cat may not grow to its full size until it is five years old.

In one old legend, the Manx was said to lose its tail when it arrived late at Noah's Ark. Noah accidentally shut the door on its tail, cutting it off completely.

Manx cats have gentle personalities. They are loyal and courageous, and may even growl to protect their owners from strangers or anything out of the ordinary.

Fact file

Originates: Isle of Man

Group: Shorthair or longhair

Height: 10–12 in./25–30 cm

Weight: 8–10 lb./3.6–4.5 kg (female); 10–12 lb./4.5–5.4 kg (male)

Color: Various

Ocicat

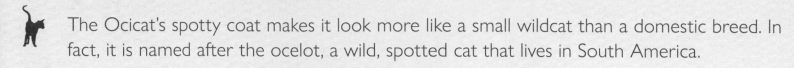

The Ocicat's spotty coat makes it look more like a small wildcat than a domestic breed. In fact, it is named after the ocelot, a wild, spotted cat that lives in South America.

Ocicats come in different colorings, but they all have the same kind of patterned coat. Their light-colored fur is sprinkled with dark spots that are shaped like thumbprints.

Each of this cat's hairs is striped in different colors, which gives its fur a speckled look. This is called "agouti" after the finely mottled fur of wild agoutis, which are related to guinea pigs.

Ocicats are one of the few cat breeds that enjoy playing with water. This is unusual, as many cats dislike getting wet.

This highly intelligent cat can easily work out how to open doors. It needs plenty of toys and activities to keep it entertained.

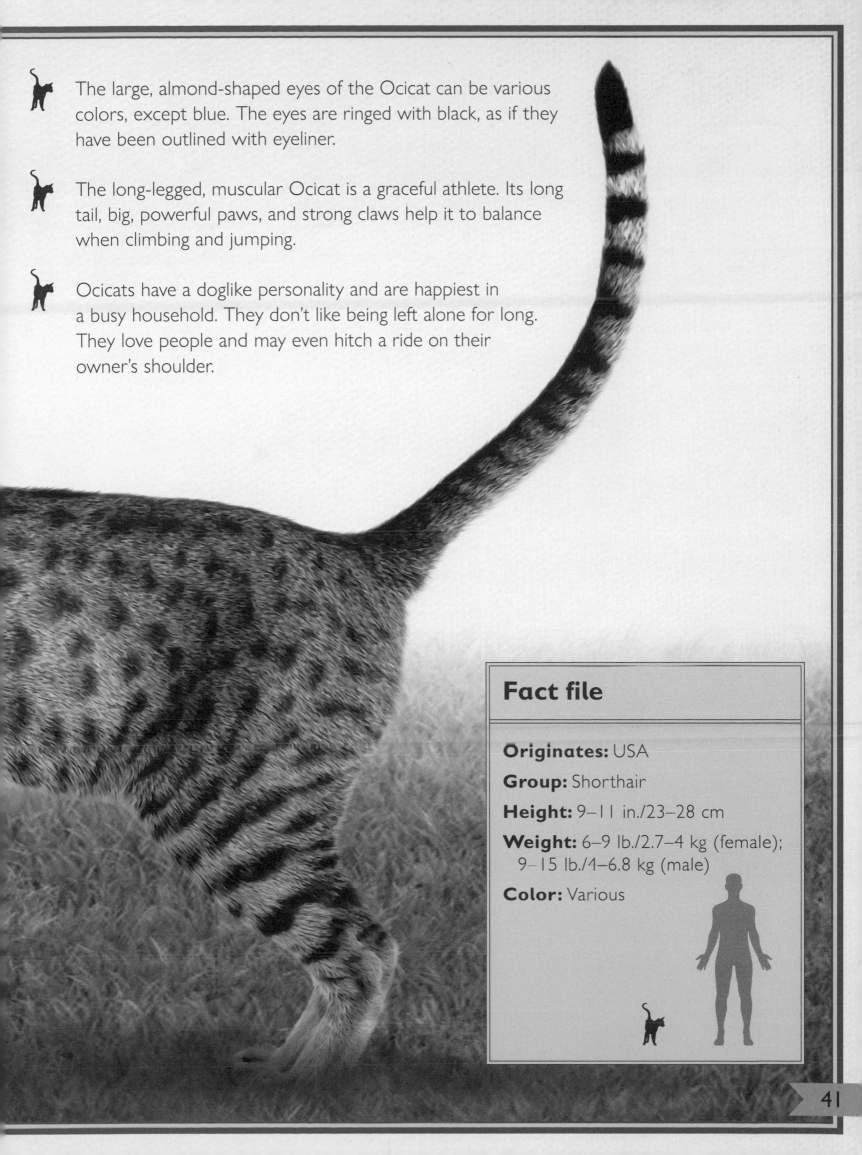

The large, almond-shaped eyes of the Ocicat can be various colors, except blue. The eyes are ringed with black, as if they have been outlined with eyeliner.

The long-legged, muscular Ocicat is a graceful athlete. Its long tail, big, powerful paws, and strong claws help it to balance when climbing and jumping.

Ocicats have a doglike personality and are happiest in a busy household. They don't like being left alone for long. They love people and may even hitch a ride on their owner's shoulder.

Fact file

Originates: USA

Group: Shorthair

Height: 9–11 in./23–28 cm

Weight: 6–9 lb./2.7–4 kg (female); 9–15 lb./4–6.8 kg (male)

Color: Various

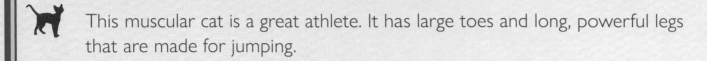

Devon Rex

This muscular cat is a great athlete. It has large toes and long, powerful legs that are made for jumping.

The Devon Rex has a curly coat like a poodle. Its fragile hair breaks easily. Its short, tightly curled whiskers and eyebrows often break off too.

The short, fine coat of a Devon Rex does not keep it very warm. It has few long, coarse outer hairs to protect its skin, so it can easily get sunburned.

This mischievous cat has a big personality. It loves to clown around, showing off all the clever tricks it has learned. The Devon Rex keeps its playful nature throughout its life.

The Devon Rex has extra-large ears. Sometimes the ears have tufts of hair inside them.

Fact file

Originates: Devon, UK

Group: Shorthair

Height: 10–12 in./25–30 cm

Weight: 5–8 lb./2–3.5 kg (female);
8–10 lb./3.5–4.5 kg (male)

Color: Various

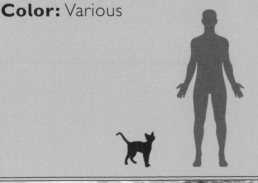

The Devon Rex's coat is not always curly all over. The fur on its head, neck, and shoulders and on its legs and paws is sometimes too short to be wavy.

Abyssinian

 An Abyssinian mother cat gives birth to about five or six kittens at a time. The kittens are full of of energy and want to play most of the time.

 Abyssinian kittens are born with darker fur than the adult cats. Their coats gradually lighten over the first few months of life.

 The high-spirited Abyssinian is sometimes called the Aby for short. It has also been nicknamed the "Aby-silly-an" because of its playful and clownlike nature.

 The Abyssinian is an amazing athlete, always running, jumping, climbing, and exploring. It can leap 6 feet (2 m) or more into the air and run at up to 30 miles per hour (48 km/h), which is faster than the world record for a human sprinter.

 The Aby's fur is short, soft, and silky and has an unusual pattern. Each hair is striped in bands of alternating light and dark color. This kind of coat pattern is known as "ticked."

 Despite its name, the Abyssinian cat does not come from Abyssinia, which is the old name for the African country of Ethiopia.

 Intelligent, curious Abyssinian cats take a keen interest in everything their owners are doing. They love being the center of attention and learn tricks quickly. They can also be taught to walk on a leash.

Fact file

Originates: Southeast Asia or northeast India

Group: Shorthair

Height: 8–10 in./20–25 cm

Weight: 6–8 lb./2.7–3.6 kg (female); 7–10 lb./3–4.5 kg (male)

Color: Various but mainly ruddy brown

45

Balinese

The Balinese cat is sometimes called "the longhaired Siamese" because it looks like a Siamese cat with very long hair. Underneath its fluffy coat, the Balinese has a long, strong body, with fine bones and lean muscles.

This slender, graceful breed was named after the elegant temple dancers on the Indonesian island of Bali, which is in Southeast Asia.

Balinese cats have a wedge-shaped head with extra-large, triangular ears and bright blue, almond-shaped eyes.

The Balinese has only a fine, silky top coat and no undercoat, so its fur does not get tangled easily. Its fur is longest on its tail, which fans out like a feather.

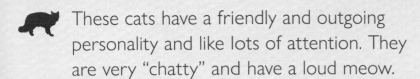 These cats have a friendly and outgoing personality and like lots of attention. They are very "chatty" and have a loud meow.

With its long, slim legs, the Balinese is an athletic and agile cat. It loves to jump, climb, explore, and play active games.

Fact file

Originates: USA, Thailand

Group: Longhair

Height: 8–13 in./20.3–33 cm

Weight: 5–7 lb./2.2–3 kg (female); 7–10 lb./3–4.5 kg (male)

Color: Usually creamy-white with darker face, ears, tail and legs

Chartreux

🐾 The Chartreux (pronounced "shar-trer") looks as if it is always smiling. This is because of the shape of the bones in its skull and jaw.

🐾 The beautiful gray-blue Chartreux has unusual water-repellent fur. If this cat gets wet, it only needs to shake itself like a dog, and its fur will be dry.

🐾 This large, muscular cat has a powerful body but is quite short in height and its legs are surprisingly skinny.

🐾 The thick fur of the Chartreux feels rather like rough sheep's wool. Its fur becomes longer and thicker in winter to keep the cat warm.

🐾 Instead of meowing, the quiet Chartreux "talks" to its owner in other ways. It will tap gently with its paw to ask to sit on its owner's lap, or bring a toy when it is ready to play.

The athletic and agile Chartreux likes to chase toys and enjoys pouncing on things. It has lightning-fast reflexes and is an expert hunter.

The famous French president Charles de Gaulle had a pet Chartreux. He was called Gris-gris, which means "gray-gray." The Chartreux is the national cat of France.

Fact file

Originates: France

Group: Shorthair

Height: 8–11 in./20–28 cm

Weight: 6–9 lb./2.7–4 kg (female); 10–14 lb./4.5–6.8 kg (male)

Color: Gray-blue

49

Japanese Bobtail

The Japanese Bobtail gets its name from its stubby, bunnylike "bobbed" tail. No two Bobtails have exactly the same-shaped tail. They are as different from each other as fingerprints are in humans.

Some Bobtails may have differently colored eyes, such as one blue and one gold.

The Bobtail is often called "the singing cat" because it uses soft, songlike meows and chirps to "talk" to its owners.

The Japanese Bobtail likes to carry things in its mouth and enjoys playing fetch or walking on a leash. It can also be trained to jump over hurdles or leap through hoops, using its long, muscular back legs.

Fact file

Originates: Japan, possibly taken there from China or Korea

Group: Shorthair or longhair

Height: 8–9 in./20–23 cm

Weight: 5–7 lb./2–3 kg (female); 7–10 lb./3–4.5 kg (male)

Color: Various

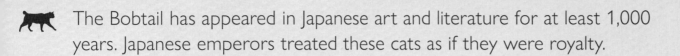 The Bobtail has appeared in Japanese art and literature for at least 1,000 years. Japanese emperors treated these cats as if they were royalty.

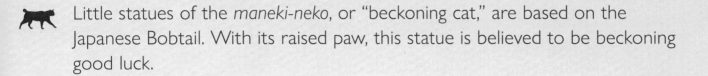 Little statues of the *maneki-neko*, or "beckoning cat," are based on the Japanese Bobtail. With its raised paw, this statue is believed to be beckoning good luck.

Brazilian Shorthair

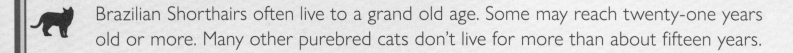

- Brazilian Shorthairs often live to a grand old age. Some may reach twenty-one years old or more. Many other purebred cats don't live for more than about fifteen years.

- This breed was developed from street cats that lived in Brazilian cities, such as Rio de Janeiro. These strays may originally have been ships' cats that Portuguese sailors brought to Brazil about 500 years ago.

- This large breed is sleek and graceful, with long, slim legs and a strong and agile body. The males tend to grow much larger than the females.

- The ears of the Brazilian Shorthair are large with rounded tips. The ears have tufts of hair inside them.

- The Brazilian Shorthair is also known as Pelo Curto Brasileiro, which means "short Brazilian hair" in Portuguese, the language of Brazil.

Fact file

Originates: Brazil

Group: Shorthair

Height: 12–14 in./30.5–35.5 cm

Weight: 8–16 lb./3.6–7.2 kg (female); 11–20 lb./5–9 kg (male)

Color: Various

This breed has a big personality. It is full of energy and loves to explore new places. The confident and friendly Brazilian Shorthair likes to be the center of attention and enjoys being around people.

Peterbald

The Peterbald is one of only six hairless cat breeds in the world. Its body may be covered with a coat of thin, velvety fuzz or wiry fur, or it may have no hair at all. Some Peterbalds don't even have whiskers or eyebrows.

A Peterbald's coat can change in the first two years of its life. Some hairless Peterbald kittens later grow fuzzy fur, while others may lose the fur they once had.

The Peterbald breed was developed in Russia. It is named after the Russian city of St. Petersburg, where it is a popular cat.

These cats have oversized, pointed ears and their almond-shaped eyes come in many colors. Their long, slim tails are shaped like whips.

Peterbalds are very sensitive to hot and cold weather. They risk getting sunburned in too much direct sunshine, and quickly feel the cold. Their delicate skin can easily get scratched and cut.

Fact file

Originates: Russia

Group: Hairless or shorthair

Height: 8–10 in./20–25 cm

Weight: 7–8 lb./3–3.8 kg (female); 9–11 lb./4–5 kg (male)

Color: Various

The almost-bare skin of a Peterbald is oilier than the skin of most other cat breeds. These cats need regular baths to stop their skin becoming sticky.

 The loyal and friendly Peterbald likes to follow its owner around, and "talks" to them a lot with its raspy voice.

Singapura

- The tiny Singapura stands only 6–8 inches (15–20 cm) tall. That's no higher than an average adult human's hand. This little cat does not reach its full size until it is about two years old.

- This breed was named after Singapura, which is the Malaysian name for Singapore. This is the city where the breed originated. Sometimes the Singapura is just called the "Pura" for short.

- The Singapura has a cream-colored chest and belly. The brown hairs on its back, legs, and tail are striped with light and dark bands, ending in a dark tip. This kind of speckled coat is known as "ticked."

- For its small size, the Singapura has big eyes and ears. Its saucer-shaped eyes are outlined in black and are either hazel, green, or yellow in color.

- The Singapura's tail is shorter than its body, and has a stubby black tip.

- The curious and intelligent Singapura has been known to open doors, drawers, and cabinets to see what is inside.

Fact file

Originates: Singapore

Group: Shorthair

Height: 6–8 in./15–20 cm

Weight: 4–6 lb./1.8–2.7 kg (female); 6–8 lb./2.7–3.6 kg (male)

Color: Brown and cream

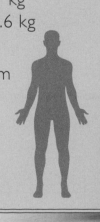

Singapura mothers usually give birth to only two or three kittens. Most cats have up to six kittens at a time, and some have as many as nine.

Singapuras have a soft, gentle voice and spend a lot of time meowing. They do not like loud noises and can easily spook if they hear a sudden, unexpected sound, or a dog barking.

Egyptian Mau

🐾 The name Mau probably comes from the ancient Egyptian word *miw*, which means "cat" or "he or she who meows."

🐾 Spotted cats similar to Egyptian Maus were worshipped in ancient Egypt. The Egyptians even had a cat-headed goddess called Bastet.

🐾 The Mau is one of the few domestic cats in the world with a naturally spotted coat. It has an M-shaped pattern of stripes on its forehead and stripes down its cheeks, a little like a modern tabby cat.

🐾 Loose skin under its belly allows the Mau to stretch its back legs out so it can sprint and leap easily.

🐾 The Egyptian Mau can spring as high as 6 feet (2 m) straight up in the air. That's as high as an adult man. It can race along as quickly as the fastest human sprinter.

🐾 The Mau has an almost musical voice. It makes meowing, chirping, whistling, and chortling sounds to communicate with its owners.

🐾 When Egyptian Maus are happy or excited, they wiggle their tails.

🐾 Egyptian Maus have light-green, almond-shaped eyes.

🐾 This breed enjoys playing in water and can even turn on taps.

Norwegian Forest Cat

The supersized Norwegian Forest Cat is as large as a small dog or a fox. Its nickname is "wegie," which is short for Norwegian.

The forest cat has its own "padded jacket" to help it survive in Norway's cold climate. Its thick, shaggy fur has a dense undercoat to help it stay snug outside. A long, coarse outer coat keeps out rain and snow.

Big, round paws with fur between the toes work like snowshoes to stop the cat from sinking into the snow. Tufted ears keep its ears warm, like earmuffs.

In spring, Norwegian Forest Cats shed their warm, downy undercoat so that they don't overheat in the summer months.

The Vikings may have taken Norwegian Forest Cats with them on their voyages to catch mice and rats on board their ships.

Fact file

Originates: Singapore

Group: Shorthair

Height: 6–8 in./15–20 cm

Weight: 4–6 lb./1.8–2.7 kg (female);
6–8 lb./2.7–3.6 kg (male)

Color: Brown and cream

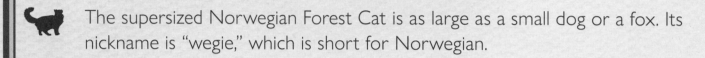

Long back legs, sturdy bodies, powerful muscles, and strong claws make wegies excellent climbers. They can even climb down trees headfirst, which many other cats cannot do.

61

Australian Mist

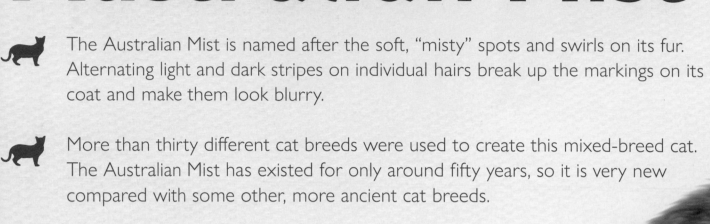

- The Australian Mist is named after the soft, "misty" spots and swirls on its fur. Alternating light and dark stripes on individual hairs break up the markings on its coat and make them look blurry.

- More than thirty different cat breeds were used to create this mixed-breed cat. The Australian Mist has existed for only around fifty years, so it is very new compared with some other, more ancient cat breeds.

- The Australian Mist was developed to be an indoor cat because many Australian states do not allow cats to roam. This helps to protect the local wildlife.

- All Australian Mists have large, expressive green eyes, which are set wide apart in their faces.

- It can take up to two years for an Australian Mist to develop its adult coat.

- The Australian Mist is Australia's national cat.

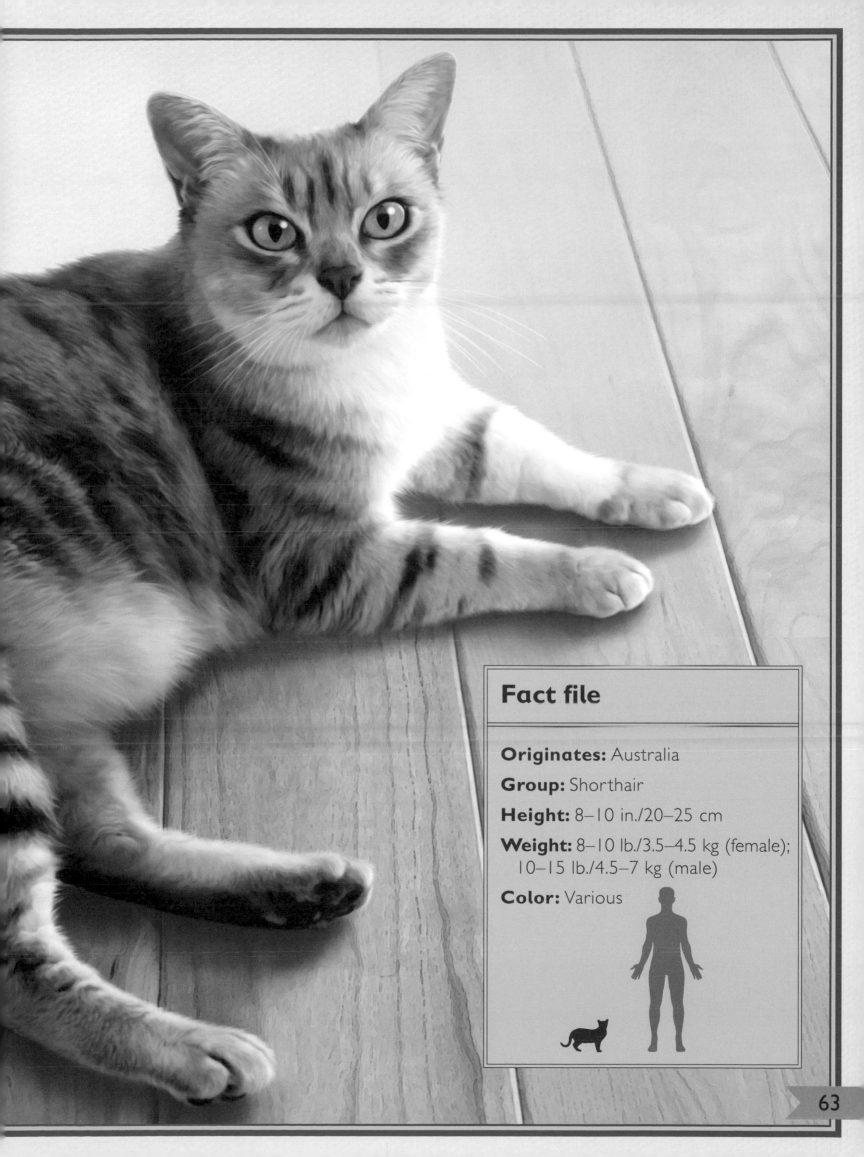

Fact file

Originates: Australia

Group: Shorthair

Height: 8–10 in./20–25 cm

Weight: 8–10 lb./3.5–4.5 kg (female);
10–15 lb./4.5–7 kg (male)

Color: Various

Lykoi

With their lean bodies, tall, pointed ears and dark gray fur, Lykois look a bit like wolves. Their name comes from the Greek word *lycos*, which means "wolf." They are also known as "werewolf cats" or "wolf cats."

Lykois shed their coat twice a year and sometimes lose all their fur. When the coat regrows, the fur may be a slightly different color. Some Lykois are completely hairless.

Lykoi kittens are born with a full coat of fluffy, solid black hair. When they are about five days old, bare patches start to form in their coats and some white hairs begin to grow among the black ones.

Sunlight and cold weather can be harmful to Lykois because of their hairless patches of pink skin. They can become sunburned if they stay out in bright sunshine for too long.

This rare breed was developed from feral cats. These are pet cats that have gone to live in the wild, rather than stay in peoples' homes.

 Although they might look rather scary, Lykois are friendly, inquisitive, playful cats. They have a gentle nature and are loving companions.

 Lykois are keen hunters and enjoy stalking their prey. When a few of them get together, they hunt their prey as a team. This is unusual, as most cats prefer to hunt alone.

Fact file

Originates: USA

Group: Shorthair

Height: 8–10 in./20–25 cm

Weight: 6–9 lb./2.7–4 kg (female); 9–12 lb./4–5.4 kg (male)

Color: Black with some white

Siamese

🐾 Siamese kittens are born with white fur. At a few weeks old, their nose, ears, paws, and tail start to darken, as if they have been dipped in colored paint. These darker tips are called "points."

🐾 The supersmart, playful, and curious Siamese likes to have lots of attention. It loves spending time with people. A pet Siamese often becomes especially close to one person.

🐾 The Siamese breed is probably more than 500 years old. The king of Siam (the old name for Thailand) had pet Siamese cats in his palace and Buddhist monks kept them in temples.

🐾 Siamese cats once had rounder faces, stockier bodies, crooked tails, and a squint in their eyes. But cat breeders slowly changed them into the sleek cats they are today.

🐾 The Siamese always tells its owners when it wants something, using a loud meow that sounds a bit like a human baby's cry.

Siamese cats are less active at night because they have trouble seeing in the dark. Unlike other cats, Siamese don't have a reflective layer at the back of their eyes to help them see in the dark.

 In Thailand, Siamese cats are called *wichien-matt*, which means "moon diamond."

Fact file

Originates: Thailand (previously known as Siam)

Group: Shorthair

Height: 8–12 in./20–31 cm

Weight: 6–10 lb./3–4.5 kg (female); 9–14 lb./4–6.4 kg (male)

Color: Creamy-colored body, brown or gray ears, face, tail, and paws

Dragon Li

This sturdy breed has been around for hundreds of years. It is one of the oldest cat breeds in the world. The Dragon Li may have developed naturally from the wild Chinese mountain cat, which lives in western China.

The Dragon Li was originally known as Li Hua Mao, which means "fox flower cat." The name comes from this cat's foxlike head and the flowerlike patterns on its coat.

The short, thick coat of the Dragon Li is made up of hairs that are black at the roots and brown at the tips. This gives the fur its unique golden-brown color.

The Dragon Li's large eyes are shaped like almonds. The eyes are usually green but may also be yellow or brown.

The Dragon Li loves to hunt and fetch things. This pet cat is also used as a working cat to catch rats in some parts of China.

An intelligent, loyal, and friendly cat, the Dragon Li is a playful and active breed. But it can demand a lot of attention from its owners.

 The Dragon Li is very rare outside China.

Fact file

Originates: China

Group: Shorthair

Height: 12–14 in./30.5–35.5 cm

Weight: 9–11 lb./4–5 kg (female); 10–12 lb./4.5–5.4 kg (male)

Color: Golden-brown tabby with broken stripes

LaPerm

- This cat is covered with bouncy, curly fur. Even its whiskers are wavy. The LaPerm's coat looks like human hair that has been permed, or treated to make it curly. That is how the breed got its name.

- A LaPerm's fur can be long or short, but it has no undercoat. Longhaired La Perms have curly, plumed tails. Shorthaired types have shorter, wavy tails shaped like round, bristly hairbrushes.

- Newborn LaPerm kittens may be bald or have short, straight, or curly hair. Most develop a curly coat when they grow up.

- This breed was developed from an American farm cat called Speedy, who gave birth to a bald kitten. By eight weeks, the kitten had grown a coat of soft curls. Later, she had her own curly-coated kittens.

- When it is relaxing, the LaPerm's eyes are almond-shaped. But they open wide and become rounder when the cat is alert.

- The LaPerms eyes come in different colors. One eye may even be a different color from the other.

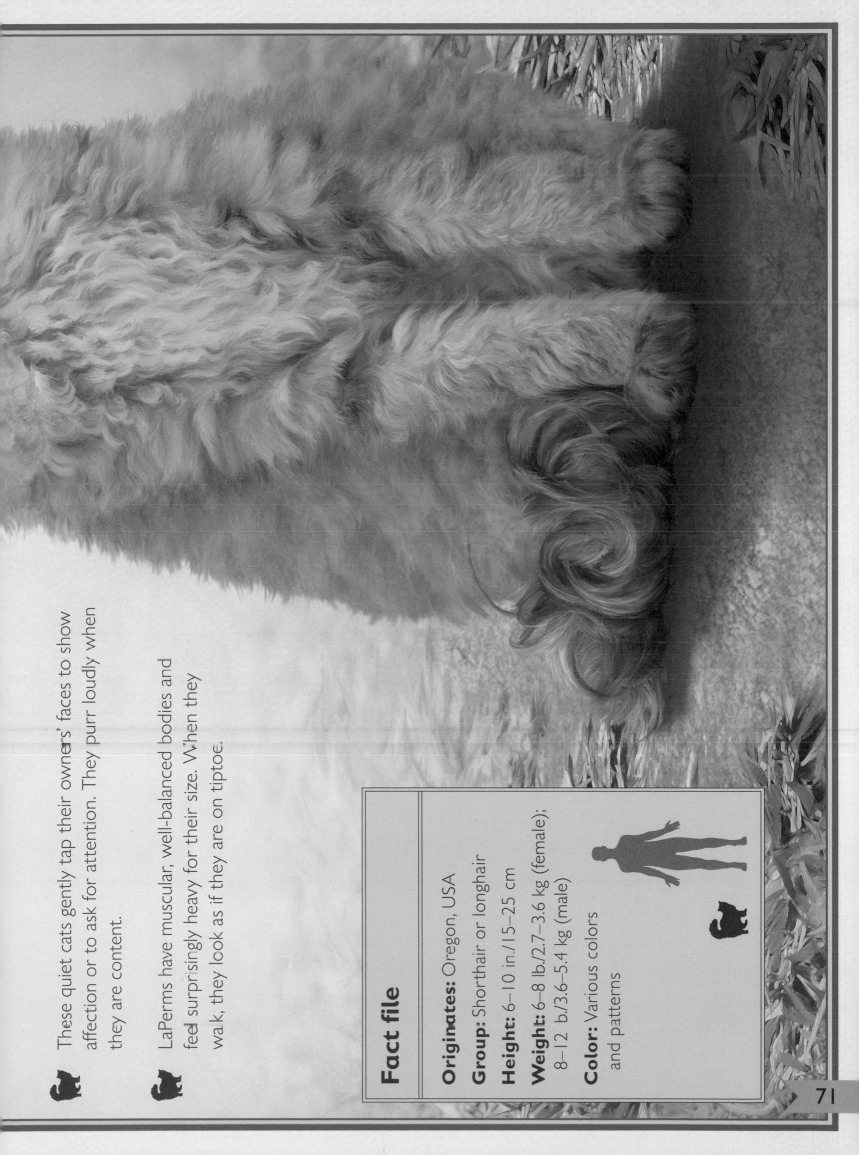

These quiet cats gently tap their owners' faces to show affection or to ask for attention. They purr loudly when they are content.

LaPerms have muscular, well-balanced bodies and feel surprisingly heavy for their size. When they walk, they look as if they are on tiptoe.

Fact file

Originates: Oregon, USA

Group: Shorthair or longhair

Height: 6–10 in./15–25 cm

Weight: 6–8 lb./2.7–3.6 kg (female); 8–12 lb./3.6–5.4 kg (male)

Color: Various colors and patterns

Havana Brown

 The sleek and glossy Havana Brown is a very rare breed. It the only cat that has brown whiskers.

 This breed is only about seventy years old. Breeders created it specially from several different cat breeds, including the Siamese. They wanted the Havana Brown to look like the brown cats that lived in Thailand hundreds of years ago.

 No one knows where the Havana's name comes from. It may be named after the deep brown color of Havana cigars. Or it may be named after the rich brown Havana rabbits from the Netherlands.

 The Havana Brown is a quiet cat with a soft meow. This smart breed uses its paws to investigate anything new, or to gently tap its owners when it wants attention.

Fact file

Originates: UK, USA

Group: Shorthair

Height: 9–11 in./23–28 cm

Weight: 6–8 lb./2.7–3.6 kg (female); 8–12 lb./3.6–5.4 kg (male)

Color: Deep brown

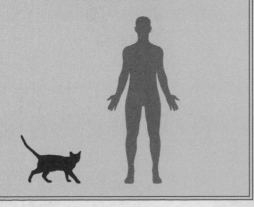

Kittens and young adult Havana Browns may have slight tabby markings, but these disappear as they grow up.

The Havana Brown always has bright green eyes, even though its Siamese ancestor usually has blue eyes.

Cats usually point their ears forward toward sounds that have caught their attention. But the Havana Brown's ears always point forward, making it look alert and interested all the time.

Scottish Fold

- The Scottish Fold is named after its unusual ears, which fold down rather than stand up straight. Its ears are very delicate.

- Scottish Folds are born with straight, pointy ears. Their ear folds usually begin to develop when the kittens are about two to four weeks old.

- With its round face and big, round eyes, this rare breed is often said to look like a teddy bear or an owl.

- The Scottish Fold uses its ears to communicate. It moves its ears back when it is afraid or angry, and moves them forward during play or when it is about to be fed.

- Scottish Folds sit, stand, and lie in unusual positions that look almost human. They may sit on their bottoms with their front paws resting on their belly. They may sleep on their backs or stand up on their back legs.

Fact file

Originates: Scotland

Group: Shorthair or longhair

Height: 8–10 in./20.3–25.4 cm

Weight: 6–9 lb./3–4 kg (female); 9–13 lb./4–6 kg

Color: Various

The eyes of some Scottish Folds are not the same color. One eye may be a different color from the other.

This cat has a sweet, gentle, easygoing personality. It is not as active and acrobatic as some other cats, so it does not spend so much time climbing and jumping.

Birman

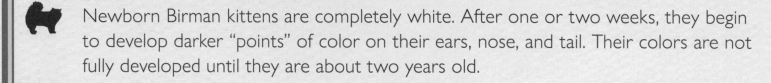

Newborn Birman kittens are completely white. After one or two weeks, they begin to develop darker "points" of color on their ears, nose, and tail. Their colors are not fully developed until they are about two years old.

The most unusual features of a Birman cat are its white feet, its sparkling, sapphire-blue eyes, and its big, bushy tail.

The name Birman comes from the French word 'Birmanie,' which means "Burma." This is the old name for Myanmar, the country where this breed originated.

An adult Birman is a large, long cat, with heavy bones and a stocky, powerful body.

Unlike many cats, the Birman doesn't like to climb and spends most of its time on the ground.

Fact file

Originates: Myanmar, France

Group: Longhair

Height: 8–10 in./20–25 cm

Weight: 6–10 lb./2.7–4.5 kg (female); 10–15 lb./4.5–6.8 kg (male)

Color: Usually creamy-white with brown nose, ears, tail and legs, and white feet

Birmans were once temple cats that were kept as loyal companions for the priests in ancient Myanmar. The Birman is sometimes known as the Sacred Cat of Burma.

 In an old legend, the first Birman is said to have been created by the goddess Tsun-Kyan-Kse. To reward a loyal temple cat, the goddess turned its white coat to creamy gold, with points of dark color. Its yellow eyes were changed to blue. But the cat's paws stayed white, as a symbol of its purity.

Common Cat

🐈 The common cat has developed naturally from the wildcats that first started living with humans thousands of years ago. It has not been specially created by people, as Siamese and other cat breeds have.

🐈 Common cats breed freely and may choose mates that look very different from themselves. This is why these cats are such a mixture of shapes, sizes, colors and patterns.

🐈 A common cat may have black, white, ginger, or gray fur. Its coat often has a striped tabby pattern, with the tabby M-shaped mark on its forehead.

🐈 Most common cats are pets, living with people in their homes.

🐈 Some common cats leave their human owners and go to live outside in towns and cities, or in the wild. Tame cats like these that have gone wild are called "feral."

🐈 The average life span of a common cat is twelve to eighteen years, although some may live as long as twenty years. The oldest common pet cat reached the grand old age of thirty-eight years.

Fact file

Originates: Worldwide

Group: Shorthair, medium-length hair, longhair

Height: 12–14 in./30–35 cm

Weight: 5–9 lb./2.5–4 kg (female); 9–12 lb./4–5.5 kg (male)

Color: Various

Cat World